E
591.5
Fis

100-10

Fisher, Ronald M.

Animals in winter.

A furry marten peers down from a branch in a pine tree.

Animals in Winter

by Ron Fisher

BOOKS FOR YOUNG EXPLORERS
NATIONAL GEOGRAPHIC SOCIETY

Brrr! The cold time of the year has come. Winter is here! A hare sits very still in the snow. The hare must find food and stay warm in winter. Winter is hard for many animals.

Snow covers the ground. Ice covers twigs and bushes that some animals eat. Food is hard to find. Not all animals look for food in the snow. Some sleep deeply in winter. This is called hibernation. Some move to warmer places where food is easier to find. This is called migration. Some make cozy homes and store food to eat in winter.

A deer does not hibernate or migrate long distances. It does not make a home or store food for the winter. The deer eats buds and twigs. It lies down to rest right in the snow. A thick winter coat helps keep the deer warm.

6

Bighorn sheep eat grass and other plants. A male bighorn, called a ram, paws the snow to get at the plants.

Look closely at this tree. A hungry moose has eaten some of the bark. In winter, moose also eat buds and twigs. In summer, they like to eat plants that grow in water. But now the water is frozen.

These animals are called pronghorns. They eat plants, too. In winter, pronghorns move to places where deep snow does not cover the plants.

A mountain lion runs through a snowy forest. Its large paws are like snowshoes. They help the big cat move over the snow.

A weasel has caught a mouse. The weasel's white winter fur blends with the snow. The weasel can sneak up on mice and other animals that it eats.

Sniff! Sniff! A red fox pokes its nose deep into the cold snow. The fox has heard a mouse and is trying to catch it.

The snow does not keep these two hungry coyotes from looking for food.

PINE SISKINS

Some people put food outside
for animals in winter.
Pine siskins, cardinals, blue jays,
and other birds may come
to your backyard if you put seeds
and fruit out for them.

A squirrel eats
kernels of corn
at a feeder.
Sitting up,
it holds the food
in its paws.

CARDINAL

BLUE JAY

Beavers have built a house called a lodge in this stream.
When ice covers the water, the beaver family usually stays inside.
The beavers eat bark from twigs they have stored underwater.
When the stream isn't frozen, they can come outside to eat.

A squirrel is living
in the hollow trunk of a tree.
A woodpecker made the hole.
The squirrel will be snug
here during the winter.

This pika will be ready
when winter comes.
The pika stores food it will eat
while the snow falls.
It gathers leaves and stems,
then puts them on rocks
near its home. They dry out
in the sun. Later the pika
will pile the dried plants
beneath the rocks.

The pika has a round body,
with short legs and ears.
Thick fur helps keep it warm.
The little pika even has fur
on the bottoms of its feet!

PIKA (say PEA-kuh or PIE-kuh)

A prairie dog comes out of its burrow on a warm winter day. Prairie dogs stay underground in bad weather.

Shhh! A ground squirrel is fast asleep in its nest. It is hibernating. It eats a lot during the summer and gets very fat. Then it curls up in a ball and goes to sleep. The animal breathes more slowly, and its heart beats more slowly. Its body temperature drops. The ground squirrel lives off its body fat until spring.

Bears are lazy in winter. They sleep and sleep and sleep. But on nice warm days they may wake up. When bears leave their dens, they sometimes sniff and scratch trees. Then they may look for food. Bears eat insects, small animals, and birds' eggs. They eat roots, berries, nuts, and honey. They eat almost anything.

During the winter, the baby bears,
called cubs, are born. In spring,
they go outside with their mother.
The cubs stay close to her.
She shows them how to hunt for food.

nimals with white coats are hard to see in the white snow. White coats help some animals hide. They help others hunt.

Polar bears are good swimmers. They live far in the north, where there is snow and ice almost all the time. The bears look like big chunks of ice. Their white coats help them sneak up on the animals they eat. A baby harp seal has white fur for only the first few weeks of its life, when it stays on the ice. Its fur will turn darker before the seal begins to swim and find food in the ocean.

A snowshoe hare does not look the same in winter as it does in summer. In winter it has white fur. In summer it has brown fur. A white coat is hard to see in winter. A brown coat is hard to see in summer. The enemies of the hares have trouble finding them.

PTARMIGAN (say TAR-mih-gun)

Birds called ptarmigans change color, too. As summer ends, a ptarmigan begins to lose its brown feathers. It grows new white ones. This change is called molting. It happens every year. The ptarmigan becomes as white as the snow. This helps protect the bird from its enemies. In the spring, it grows brown feathers again.

Insects lead short, busy lives. Most live only a few months. In late summer, a praying mantid lays her eggs inside an egg case. The strong case protects the eggs all winter long. Snow and ice usually cannot harm them.

When winter is over, baby praying mantids hatch. These mantids are climbing along a twig near their egg case. They are very small. They begin eating tiny insects, and they grow and grow until the end of summer. Then the females will lay eggs just as their mother did, and die before cold weather comes.

Warm weather
is here at last.
Flowers are blooming.
The sun feels warm,
and the breeze feels
fresh. A young deer
called a fawn has
a spotted coat that
blends with flowers.
In late summer,
the fawn will grow
a gray coat like
its mother's.

ELK

MOUNTAIN GOAT

In spring, some animals molt. They lose their heavy winter coats and
grow lighter summer ones. A bull elk is growing a new summer coat.
It will be a pretty reddish color. His new antlers are covered
with soft skin called velvet. They will grow all summer long.
A mountain goat sheds his winter coat. Big clumps of hair fall off.

A watchful mother sheep and her newborn baby rest on a mountainside. The lamb is only a few days old. During the summer it will grow. It will nibble grass and other plants. It will play in the sun with other lambs. It will leap from rock to rock and climb near the cliffs where it lives. The lamb will begin to grow horns. It will be bigger and stronger before winter comes again.

Published by The National Geographic Society
Gilbert M. Grosvenor, *President;* Melvin M. Payne, *Chairman of the Board;*
Owen R. Anderson, *Executive Vice President;* Robert L. Breeden, *Vice President,*
Publications and Educational Media

Prepared by The Special Publications Division
Donald J. Crump, *Director*
Philip B. Silcott, *Associate Director*
William L. Allen, William R. Gray, *Assistant Directors*

Staff for this Book
Margery G. Dunn, *Managing Editor*
Charles E. Herron, *Picture Editor*
Marianne R. Koszorus, *Art Director*
Palmer Graham, *Researcher*
Katheryn M. Slocum, *Illustrations Assistant*

Engraving, Printing, and Product Manufacture
Robert W. Messer, *Manager;* George V. White, *Production Manager*
Mary A. Bennett, David V. Showers, *Production Project Managers;* Mark R. Dunlevy, Richard A. McClure, Gregory Storer, *Assistant Production Managers*
Katherine H. Donohue, *Senior Production Assistant;* Katherine R. Leitch, *Production Staff Assistant*

Nancy F. Berry, Pamela A. Black, Nettie Burke, Claire M. Doig, Rosamund Garner, Victoria D. Garrett, Sheryl A. Hoey, Virginia A. McCoy,
Cleo Petroff, Victoria I. Piscopo, Tammy Presley, Carol A. Rocheleau, Jenny Takacs, Carole L. Tyler, *Staff Assistants*

Consultants
Dr. Glenn O. Blough, Judith Hobart, *Educational Consultants;* Lynda Ehrlich, *Reading Consultant*
Dr. Richard W. Coles, Director, Washington University Tyson Research Center; Dr. Henry W. Setzer, Curator of Mammals, Emeritus,
Smithsonian Institution, *Scientific Consultants*

Illustrations Credits
Stephen J. Krasemann, DRK PHOTO (cover, 4, 8-9, 10 lower, 30-31); Leonard Lee Rue III, ANIMALS ANIMALS (1, 5); Mark Tomalty, MASTERFILE (2-3, 16); David C. Fritts, ANIMALS ANIMALS (6-7 upper, 24 upper left); Harry Engels (6-7 lower, 7, 17 upper, 17 lower, 28 left); Wayne Lankinen (10 upper); Annie Griffiths (11); Jen & Des Bartlett, BRUCE COLEMAN INC. (13 upper left); S. Osolinski, FREELANCE PHOTOGRAPHERS GUILD (12-13); National Geographic Photographer Bates Littlehales (12); Laura Riley, BRUCE COLEMAN INC. (13 upper right); Wolfgang Bayer, BRUCE COLEMAN INC. (14 lower left); Harry Engels, NATIONAL AUDUBON SOCIETY COLLECTION/ PHOTO RESEARCHERS, INC. (14 lower right); John L. Ebeling (14-15); Jeff Foott, BRUCE COLEMAN INC. (18-19); S. C. Kaufman, NASC/PR (19); J. Van Wormer, BRUCE COLEMAN INC. (20-21); Wayne Lankinen, DRK PHOTO (21 upper); Stephen J. Krasemann, PETER ARNOLD, INC. (21 lower); Janet Foster, MASTERFILE (22); MASTERFILE (22-23); Ray Richardson, ANIMALS ANIMALS (24 lower left); Brian Milne, ANIMALS ANIMALS (24 right); Stephen J. Krasemann, BRUCE COLEMAN INC. (24-25); Lee Battaglia, NASC/PR (26-27); George D. Lepp, BRUCE COLEMAN INC. (26 left); Ken Lewis, ANIMALS ANIMALS (26 right); Kenneth W. Fink, BRUCE COLEMAN INC. (28 right); Tom and Pat Leeson (28-29); Jim Brandenburg (32).

This is a prairie dog town, but where are all the prairie dogs? They are underground. They stay there while the snow piles high above them.

Cover: A spruce cone makes a mouthful for a red squirrel. The squirrel will eat the seeds inside it.

Library of Congress CIP Data
Fisher, Ronald M.
  Animals in winter.

  (Books for young explorers)
  Summary: Describes how animals face the rigors of winter by hibernating, migrating, storing food, or changing colors to blend with the winter landscape.
  1. Animals—Wintering—Juvenile literature. [1. Animals—Habits and behavior. 2. Winter]
I. Title. II. Series.
QL753.F55 1982   591.5'43   82-47859
ISBN 0-87044-453-0